HUNTING

SHARKS

in L. Nelson

⌐ Lerner Publications Company • Minneapolis

This book is available in two editions:
Library binding by Lerner Publications Company, a division of Lerner Publishing Group
Soft cover by First Avenue Editions, an imprint of Lerner Publishing Group
241 First Avenue North
Minneapolis, MN 55401

Website address: www.lernerbooks.com

Words in *italic* type are explained in a glossary on page 30.

Library of Congress Cataloging-in-Publication Data

Nelson, Kristin L.
    Hunting sharks / by Kristin L. Nelson.
        p.   cm. — (Pull ahead books)
    Summary: Introduces the behavior, physical characteristics, and life cycle of the shark.
    ISBN: 0–8225–4671–X (lib. bdg. : alk. paper)
    ISBN: 0–8225–3648–X (pbk. : alk. paper)
        1. Sharks—Juvenile literature. [1. Sharks.] I. Title. II. Series.
    QL638.9 .N45 2003
    597.3—dc21   2002007935

Manufactured in the United States of America
1 2 3 4 5 6 — JR — 08 07 06 05 04 03

Sharks are good hunters.
What is this shark hunting?

This shark is
hunting a
fur seal.

Chomp! The shark sinks its teeth
into the seal.

Sharks are *predators*.

Predators are animals that hunt and eat other animals.

This shark is eating a bird.

The bird is the shark's *prey*. Prey is an animal that is hunted for food.

Sharks eat many different kinds of animals.

Sharks eat sea turtles.

Sharks eat squid. Sharks also eat
octopuses and crabs.

How would you find food if you
were a shark?

A shark's sense of hearing helps it find animals.

It can hear an animal
from miles away.

A shark's sense of smell helps it hunt.

The two holes above this shark's mouth are nostrils. Sharks smell with their nostrils.

Most sharks have good eyesight
to help them find food.

This shark can see animals
that are in front of it or beside it.

Sharks also use tiny pores
to sense the movement of animals.

A shark's pores are on its head.

Sharks have sharp teeth. Here are the teeth of a great white shark.

When a shark finds prey, it opens its jaws and bites down.

This sand tiger shark has many rows
of teeth. If it loses a tooth,
the tooth will grow back.

Some teeth grow back in one day.

Did you know sharks have teeth on their skin, too?

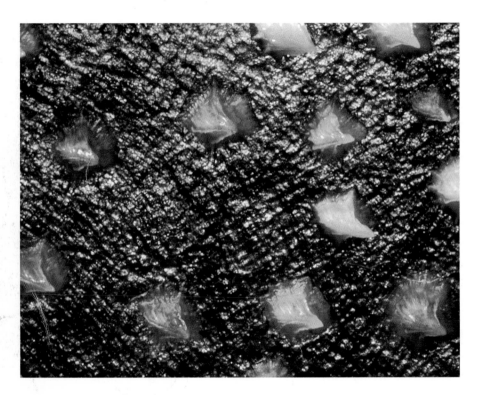

These teeth are tiny, rough scales called *denticles*.

Denticles help water flow over
a shark's body when it swims.

Why does this shark swim
with its mouth open?

A shark swims with its mouth open so it can breathe. The water goes into its mouth and flows over its *gills.*

Gills are slits behind a shark's eyes.

Fins help sharks to move
and to steer.

The side fins are called *pectoral fins*.
They help the shark to go up or down.

The two fins on top of a shark's body are called *dorsal fins.*

They keep the shark from rolling over.

The tail fin is called the *caudal fin*.
It helps the shark to move forward.

This female shark swims to a safe
place to give birth to her babies.

Baby sharks are called *pups.*

Most pups start as eggs that grow inside the mother. Some pups grow for one year before they are born.

When it is time, the pups swim out of their mother's body.

This shark is giving birth to a baby.

Some mother sharks lay their eggs on the ocean floor.

The eggs are protected by *egg cases.*

This pup is coming out of its
egg case.

Shark pups are ready to swim and
hunt as soon as they are born.

Small pups can become big sharks.
This shark will be up to 12 feet long.

That is as long as a small car!

Sharks are the most powerful
hunters in the ocean!

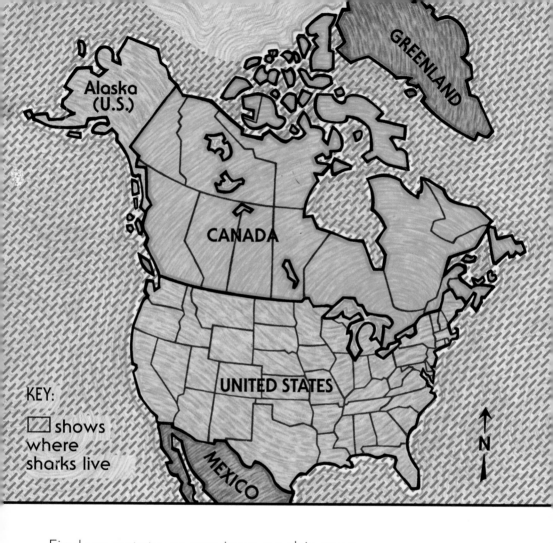

KEY:

☐ shows where sharks live

Alaska (U.S.)

GREENLAND

CANADA

UNITED STATES

MEXICO

N

Find your state or province on this map.
Do sharks live near you?

Parts of a Shark's Body

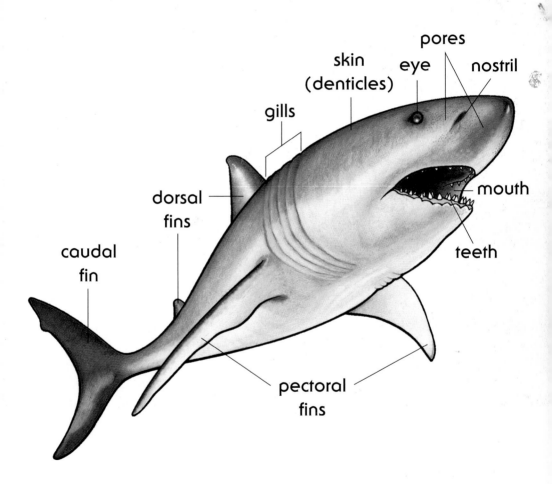

pores

skin
(denticles)

eye

nostril

gills

mouth

dorsal
fins

teeth

caudal
fin

pectoral
fins

Glossary

caudal fin: a shark's tail fin. The caudal fin moves from side to side to help a shark move forward.

denticles: tiny, rough scales on a shark's skin

dorsal fins: the two fins on top of a shark's body

egg cases: small sacs that protect a mother shark's eggs on the ocean floor

gills: slits above a shark's two side fins. The shark uses its gills to breathe.

pectoral fins: fins on a shark's side that help it to go up or down

predators: animals that hunt and eat other animals

prey: animals that are hunted by other animals

pups: baby sharks

Hunt and Find

- a shark **catching food** on pages 5–7.

- a shark's **egg case** on pages 24–25.

- a shark **pup** on pages 23, 25, 26.

- a shark's **teeth** on pages 14–15.

- a shark **leaping** out of the water on pages 4–5.

- a shark's **fins** on pages 19–21.

About the Author

Denny Pederson

Kristin L. Nelson loves writing books for children. Along with sharks, she has written about several other animals for Lerner's Pull Ahead series. When she's not working on a book, Kristin likes to read, sing jazz, walk, and bike. She lives in Savage, Minnesota, with her husband, Bob, and son, Ethan.

Photo Acknowledgments

The photographs in this book are reproduced with the permission of: © Jeremy Stafford-Deitsch/Seapics.com, front cover; © David B. Fleetham/Tom Stack & Associates, p. 3; © C & M Fallows/Seapics.com, pp. 4, 5; © Mark Conlin/Seapics.com, pp. 6, 24, 25; © Tim Clark/Seapics.com, p. 7; © Masa Ushioda/Seapics.com, pp. 8, 11, 19; © Bob Cranston/Seapics.com, p. 9; © David B. Fleetham/Seapics.com, pp. 10, 20; Phillip Colla/Seapics.com, pp. 12, 13; © James D. Watt/Seapics.com, pp. 14, 26, 27; © Ross Isaacs/Seapics.com, p. 15; © Doug Perrine/Jose Castro/Seapics.com, p. 16; © Amos Nachoum /Seapics.com, pp. 17, 31, © Doug Perrine/Seapics.com, pp. 18, 21, 22, 23.